Puffin Books

Sister

Tom's small sister Annie blames all her
mischief on her imaginary friend, a tiny,
red-haired, volatile, disruptive mite called
Sister, who bullies and torments the entire
family.

And then the usually practical, unimaginative
Tom is overcome by a dreadful suspicion – he
begins to think Sister might be real. But how
can he force the tiny terrorist to reveal herself
to the rest of the family?

Is the solution to Tom's dilemma hidden in
the long-running science-fiction comic strip
drawn by his older brother Jack?

Before the answer is revealed, some very
strange things happen...

Also by Joan Flanagan

The Dingbat Spies

Rose Terrace

The Squealies

Blinks

The Ghost in the Gazebo

Mr Shanahan's Secret

Joan Flanagan

SISTER

with illustrations by Bill Wood

Puffin Books
Penguin Books Australia
487 Maroondah Highway, PO Box 257
Ringwood, Victoria, 3134, Australia
Penguin Books Ltd
Harmondsworth, Middlesex, England
Viking Penguin Inc.
40 West 23rd Street, New York, NY 10010, USA
Penguin Books Canada Limited
2801 John Street, Markham, Ontario, Canada, L3R 1B4
Penguin Books (N.Z.) Ltd
182–190 Wairau Road, Auckland 10, New Zealand

First published by Penguin Books Australia, 1988

Typeset in Century Old Style by Dudley E. King Pty Ltd.
Made and printed in Australia by Australian Print Group, Maryborough

Flanagan, Joan, 1931–
Sister
ISBN 0 14 032827 0.
I. Wood, Bill. II. Title.
A823′.3

For Clare Flanagan,
my sister and very good friend.

1

I could hear the screeching as soon as I got to our front gate.

It had been Mrs Silver's turn to fetch us all from school and she waited till I went through the gate before starting up her car. She didn't seem to have heard the noise coming from our house.

Mum's voice was the loudest, but Annie's was in there too.

Annie's only three. She's okay for a girl. *You* know, not too much trouble. But – as dad often says – she can make more noise than a ten-year-old. The last time he said that, mum asked, 'A ten-year-old what?' He thought for a bit and then said, 'Oh... well, let's say a ten-year-old road drill.'

On top of the mother-squeals, and the yelling of the very loud child, I could hear the squawks of Walter (he's dad's old, cranky, white cockatoo).

In our house, that kind of rumpus usually means one thing. Yes, it just had to be that *Sister* was up to her tricks again.

I'd better tell you at once that Sister isn't a real person. She's Annie's invisible friend – you know, nobody else but Annie can see her. Of course, the way Sister carries on, nobody else really wants to.

The way Annie tells it, Sister causes a whole lot of trouble. If there's a doll's pram left out in the driveway, then Sister left it there. If there are towels all over the bathroom floor, then Sister threw them there. Sticky lollies stuck to the seats of the car? Sister strikes again!

Annie told me that Sister is about fifteen centimetres high. Annie doesn't know what a centimetre is, of course. The way she explained it to me was this: 'Sister is a bit bigger than your warrior dolls, but not as fat. She doesn't like the warrior dolls, she says they look dopey. Sister says what do you have dopey little fat boy dolls like that for? Sister thinks ...' And so on, and so on. I won't tell you all the stuff Sister thinks because I guess you're like me and feel that Sister ought to keep her nose out of other people's toy bins.

It's no good saying, 'Well, then, what does the little pest look like?' because the freaky thing about Sister is that she seems to look exactly like Annie. Red hair tied back in two bunches, the same yucky white face. She's skinny, like Annie, too.

And if somebody says, 'And what is this Sister person wearing today?' Annie will always describe exactly what she is wearing herself. Mum tried to ask her about this – 'Do you and Sister have a little talk every morning and pick out what you're going to wear?' – but Annie only shook her head. It seems nobody, but *nobody,* tells Sister what to wear. Or what to eat. Or what to say. Or what to do. Or how to behave.

I think Annie is hoping to be able to get away with that kind of thing herself.

I stood by the gate, thinking. It's never a good idea to rush into the house when the people in it are making a great deal of noise because, as dad has explained to me, 'At a time like that, you only have to open your mouth and say one thing and – abracadabra, lo and behold – suddenly they all become best friends again, and then they start blaming you for the whole noisy shout-up.'

It seemed to be a good idea to go around to the side of the house and peep in the window of the family room. But when I did do that it was very difficult to work out what was going on.

Mum was dashing about, and she looked very upset. Now, that isn't a bit like her. She's usually pretty quiet; she speaks very softly and slowly, she *explains* things, a lot, to us kids. In fact, she gets so used to talking to people our size that sometimes, when she's talking to grown ups, she forgets they know as much about things as she does, and she starts explaining things to *them.* Dad teases her about the time she was sitting next to this really big-deal client of his, some old person from the sailing club, it was. Dad was trying to sell him one of the boats he builds. 'Not only did you tell the Commodore how to look right, then left, then right again before he crosses a street, Roz, but you cut his meat up as well.'

Well, good old quiet mum had blown her top this time. She was leaping around, shouting instructions to Annie. 'Get them! Catch them in your fingers! Don't let them get away!' And she was waving a saucepan around. As I watched her, she whirled about, spotted something on the wall and thumped the saucepan down on the spot...Then yelled 'Yahhhhhh!' and swooped off again.

Annie wasn't being much help. She just stood there, watching, her hands clasped behind her back.

Walter, the cocky, was extremely interested in the carry-on. He likes a bit of noise. He had his head on one side and his big beak poked through the bars of his cage. He was twisting his head, the way he does, to get a better look with one eye. He was talking in his friendly way. 'G'day, Roz! Cup of tea, Roz?' He calls mum Roz. I guess he's heard dad calling her that.

Suddenly, I saw what the trouble was. Dad's budgies had got loose. They're tiny blue birds, and they seem to be frightened of everything and everyone. They don't talk and chatter and make a row, like Walter. Mostly, they just cuddle up together in their cage and worry. They're real wimps, those budgies. The biggest excitement in their cage is when one of them makes a mistake and bumps into the bell. Dad says if they ever do speak, as most budgies do, they won't shout out cheeky stuff like Walter does. The most they'll do is whisper 'Sorry!'

One of them was perching high on a shelf, and the other was doing a quick swoop across the room to join him. As I looked down towards the floor, I saw the cat, Ginger, sitting looking at them. Ginger had that 'here comes my dinner!' look on his face. I thought maybe I'd better get busy and save those budgies.

'Tom!' said mum. 'Oh thank goodness! Quickly, climb up and get the birds!'

It was easy to climb up to the top shelf of that dresser. Gosh, it ought to be. I've been going up there since I was three years old. That's where they keep the biscuit barrel.

'Go carefully!' said mum. 'Mind those cups and saucers! Here, do you want the saucepan?'

But I didn't need the saucepan. I knew if I stretched out my finger in front of the birds, and held it steady just under their tummies, they would step onto it and let me bring them down. Mum knows that, too, of course, but she doesn't like the feel of their little, skinny claws.

I guess they were glad to see me, I could see their little chests fluttering – I guess they'd seen Ginger licking his lips, too.

Mum said, 'Now, go quietly, Tom! Don't frighten them!' That was good! After she'd scared them out of their wits by chasing them with a saucepan!

I picked them up one at a time, and brought them carefully down to where mum had their cage ready.

'Thank goodness!' She shot the little bolt across and then turned around on Annie. But, being such a good mother, she suddenly seemed to choke back on the temper. You could tell she was as mad as blazes, but she was going to be reasonable, or else.

But Annie didn't wait for mum to explain why it is not a nice thing to let birds out of their cages.

She'd heard that sort of thing before, anyway. 'I didn't do it,' she said firmly, 'Sister did!'

'Now then, Annie,' said mum softly, 'You know that is not true. You opened that cage yourself.'

'No,' said Annie, looking mum straight in the eye. 'Sister did.'

'We know, don't we, that if I hadn't been here, Ginger might have caught the birds, and eaten them?'

'No,' said Annie. 'Tom got them down.'

'But what if Tom hadn't been able to . . .'

'Yes,' said Annie. 'He always does.' I thought she looked a little disappointed. 'Anyway, Sister doesn't like the budgies.'

That was a new one. Of course, there are a lot of things Sister doesn't like – muesli, peanut butter, pumpkin, being told not to put things in the supermarket trolley, having to wear a raincoat, or pick up toys, being told where to sit in the car (she likes to ride on dad's head, but he says it makes him twitchy to think of her, perched up there), hearing dad say 'Fasten your seatbelts!'

'Your father is very fond of those birds,' said mum. 'Sister says he never talks to them now,' said Annie. 'She says he did when he first got them, but now he's forgotten all about them. Sister says he's sick of them.'

'Yes,' I said. 'And we're sick of her. Is there anything to eat, mum?'

'Make yourself a peanut-butter sandwich,' said

mum, going off to dad's workroom. Before he builds his boats, he does drawings of them in this little building in the garden; and he likes us to stay out of there while he's doing it. But I guess mum thought he ought to hear about the terrible danger his birds had been in.

I called after her, 'Tell him who came to the rescue!' and then I turned to Annie, who was watching me hopefully. She's not allowed to make her own sandwiches, and I suppose she knew she didn't have much chance of getting one from mum just then. 'You did that yourself, didn't you?'

She stared at me.

'You let those birds out.'

'No, Sister did. Sister said those little budgies are dumb. She says they just sit there all day. She says they should learn tricks like Walter. She says they should talk like Walter does. She says ... '

'Where is she now?' I asked. 'Where is old Sister?'

'Standing on your shoulder,' said Annie.

Now that caught me by surprise. I couldn't stop myself patting my right shoulder.

'No' said Annie. 'The other side. She says to tell you she's on the other side.'

But she didn't catch me that time.

'Oh yes,' I said, unscrewing the peanut butter. 'And what's she doing?'

'She's staring into your ear,' said Annie.

Yuck! She caught me again. I slapped my hand to my left ear.

'Ha!' said Annie. 'Sister got you! She got you that time! She's really pleased. She says ... '

'Annie, there isn't any Sister, is there?'

But she just stood there staring at me, and staring at the bread and butter, and staring at the strawberry jam (she's gone off peanut butter since Sister got a hate on it) and, well, what can you do with a three-year-old kid who's starving in front of your eyes?

I made her a jam sandwich.

But I wouldn't make one for Sister! Annie says Sister can undo cages and throw towels about in the bathroom, so let her make her own sandwiches!

2

'Sister must go!' said mum, banging a saucepan lid down. 'There isn't room in this house for the two of us!'

I was surprised to hear that; it's quite a big house.

'Now, then, Jane,' dad was sitting on the sofa in the family room, with a mug of coffee, 'you're talking about Sister as though she were real.'

'Hmmmmm,' said mum. I looked at her quickly. Was she beginning to think Sister *was* real?

'Now,' he continued, 'if we take no notice of this Sister talk, Annie will gradually forget about it.'

'No, she won't,' I said. 'If Annie forgets about Sister, she won't have anyone to blame for all the bad things she does.'

'Ah,' said dad, 'Annie could just stop doing bad things.'

I thought about that for a bit. 'She won't like that idea.'

He was beginning to look annoyed. 'Perhaps

she'll like it a little bit better after she's had a couple of good hard whacks.'

That set mum off. 'There is no need to smack children,' she said. 'All we have to do is explain to them why it is nicer for everyone if they are good.'

'Fine,' said dad. 'Then kindly explain to Annie that it would be nicer for me if the budgies were left in their cage.'

'You already did that, mum,' I said.

'Well, then,' said dad, 'we have tried the kindly way. I would ask, you, Roz, to explain *now* to Annie that the next time the budgies get out she will get the very dickens of a whack.'

'But Annie believes that Sister let the budgies out,' said mum. 'Therefore, she will think that Sister should get the whack.'

'You'd never catch Sister, mum!'

'No,' she said, 'she certainly seems to move very quickly.'

'Now you two are doing it!' said dad. 'You're talking as though Sister were real.'

I hadn't realized I'd started to do that. I don't really think mum had noticed she was doing it either.

'Roz?' he said.

But she didn't seem to hear him.

He sighed and picked up the saucepan mum had used in the big budgie hunt. 'Here, Roz, take this and see if you can catch her.' He was teasing mum, I knew.

But it didn't seem to bother mum. She sighed. 'I don't think I could chase Sister with a saucepan,' she said.

'Don't worry about it, mum,' I said. 'I don't think you could catch her with a saucepan!'

'Tom, Tom!' Dad was shaking his head. 'You're disappointing me. You're the only sensible child we have. The only one who has never trotted out an invisible friend.'

I thought about that for a bit. 'You mean Jack had an invisible friend?' That was hard to believe. Jack is twelve.

He plays footy and rides a skateboard. Although he spends a lot of time drawing this comic strip he made up, somehow I can't imagine him sitting about talking to tiny little people nobody else can see.

'Used to!' said dad, cheerfully. 'When he was small. Surely, Roz, you remember what we went through with Mudman.'

Mum smiled. 'Heavens, I'd forgotten Mudman! Mudman certainly caused a lot of trouble in his day.'

'Who was Mudman?' I asked.

'Well, he was . . .' Mum had to think for a bit. 'I suppose he was about the same size as Sister, but Jack said you could never know exactly what he looked like because he was always covered in mud. It was all over his boots, all over his body, and he even had mud plastered all over his head.'

'Why?'

'Because,' dad smiled, 'when Jack was very small, he couldn't imagine anything nicer than being allowed to go about all day, covered in yucky, slimy mud.'

'He still likes it,' I said, thinking of the last time I'd seen Jack coming off the footy field.

'Was Mudman a pest like Sister?'

'Worse,' said dad. 'A lot worse. He was always getting thrown out with the garbage, or left behind when we went on a picnic. I've driven all over the district looking for Mudman.'

'I don't think you minded,' said mum. 'I think you *liked* Mudman.'

'Oh well,' said dad, 'he did some cheeky things. Do you remember when Jack tried to paint Walter's feathers with your nail varnish? That was Mudman's idea, as I recall...and then the day when...'

I left them chattering on about daring, marvellous Mudman as I made my way to the room I share with Jack. I found him drawing his comic strip. He really loves drawing it. When you see Jack sitting down, you can be sure you'll see him busy sketching away in the little squares.

The comic is about a star fleet whizzing around the galaxies. Mum says if someone didn't stop Jack he'd cover every piece of paper in the house with strips and strips of drawings for his comic strip. I think he would like to cover every piece of paper in the galaxy.

I sat and watched him for a bit. He's certainly good at it. 'How is Telquark?' I asked. Telquark is his big hero. Telquark is the captain of the star fleet. Telquark is an earthling; he's five thousand years old. He spends a lot of time fighting some creatures called Trogs.

The really interesting thing about Telquark is that he never had to go to school. Jack says Telquark didn't have to be taught to read or write or to find his way through the galaxies; he just *knows* things.

But maybe Telquark doesn't know absolutely everything because suddenly Jack said, 'He's having trouble landing on this new planet he's found.'

'Can't you just beam him down?'

Jack looked disgusted. He didn't answer that; he just kept drawing.

I waited a bit more and then hit him with the big

question that was troubling me. 'Jack, what happened to Mudman?'

There was no answer. His coloured pen was whizzing across the paper.

'Mudman, Jack! Where did he go?' Well, he must have gone somewhere, because he wasn't in the house with us now. I thought if I could find out how they got rid of Mudman, we might be able to do the same thing to get rid of pesky old Sister.

After a bit, Jack stopped drawing, and sat looking at me. 'Who were you talking about?'

'Mudman,' I said.

'I don't know him.' He said that, but somehow he looked a bit bothered.

I wandered over to the playtable and picked up a bit of Lego.

'Don't go messing with that,' said Jack. He's building me a space station. It looks very like the one Telquark lives in when he's home on earth. I suspect Jack really wants to build it for himself but he thinks people will laugh at a boy of twelve playing with Lego.

'Can I help?' After all, it is my space station.

'Oh, all right,' Jack looked up. 'That bit over near the edge. That's the rocks where the cave people hide when they're watching the space ships land. You can work on that.'

It wasn't as good as having a go at the control tower, or the building that hid the Trogblaster missiles, but at least it was something. I worked away for a bit on the rocks, but somehow they all came out looking like a pile of Lego blocks.

I went back to take a look at the Comic Strip Adventures of Telquark. 'I see you got him down,' I said.

And then something in the last strip of pictures made me sit up straight. 'Who's that?' I asked, pointing to a strange creature who was standing watching as Telquark poked his head up out of the little lid on top of his spacecraft. It wasn't a Trog, of course. If it had been a Trog, it would have been hiding behind a rock and hoping the alien space-craft would magically self destruct. No, the new person was a strange, brown, messy-looking man, with something dripping from his arms and legs. His head was covered in what...
looked...like...*mud*!

Jack gave a little jump. 'Oh,' he said, 'that's what the people on the new planet look like.'

Well, that's what he said, but he didn't fool me. Jack had drawn Mudman. When I thought about it, I remembered seeing that creature in the comic strip before. So he had really seen him when he was little, and he *hadn't* forgotten what he looked like! I guess he'd stopped talking about him because, now that he was twelve, he was too old, really, to have an imaginary friend.

What have I said! Of course, Jack still had imaginary friends – Telquark and the Trogs – only now he didn't talk to them and carry them around with him, and leave them behind at picnic grounds. *Now* they all lived in his comic strip.

And there was Annie starting off on the same game (it was *rather* like a game). She insisted she could see Sister, and was always carrying her about and talking to her.

It didn't seem very fair. Why hadn't I ever had an invisible playmate? I wondered was ten too old to find your very own imaginary person? I wondered would I ever have my own comic strip?

I went back to the family room. It was warm there. Mum was in the kitchen part of the room, singing with the radio the way she does. I settled down on the sofa and stared at the television set.

'You can turn it on,' said mum, reaching to switch off her transistor. We're not supposed to watch television before five o'clock but I suppose she's noticed I was feeling a bit sad.

After watching some dopey game where people

won boyfriends as prizes, I went over and climbed up on one of the stools that are lined up beside the big bench that divides the cooking part of the room from the living part.

'Mum,' I said.

'Mmmmmm . . .' She was chopping up carrots. She gave me a bit to chew. I guess she thought that was some kind of treat. Mum's always hoping we'll really get to like healthy food.

'Mum, why didn't I ever have an invisible friend?'

She understood at once the way I was feeling. 'Oh Tom. All children are different. Jack and Annie now, they like to imagine things. But you! Well you have a very special gift. You see things exactly as they are!'

I couldn't see anything special about that, for goodness sake.

'You're a practical boy. You can fix things. You can programme the video for me. You can catch the budgies when they get loose. It was you who got Ginger down from the roof when she got herself stuck up there.'

Huh! Anyone could rescue a dopey cat!

But I guess what mum had said made me feel a little bit better.

There was something else I wanted to ask her. 'Mum, have you ever thought that Sister might be real?'

Mum looked startled. 'Well, no, of course not,'

said mum. She didn't sound absolutely sure, though. 'Annie has simply imagined Sister. She...'

'No. I asked Annie did she make Sister up, but she says no she didn't. She says Sister is real! She could be right, mum.'

'Tom! Don't even say it!'

'Dad doesn't think she is, though.'

But that was *possibly* about to change. Suddenly, the back door slammed and dad rushed in. He was really mad. His face was all red, and his eyes were big and they seemed to be sort of popping out a bit from his head. 'She's gone too far!' he shouted. 'This time Sister has gone too far!'

'Now, then, Bill, what????' but mum got no further.

'She's got into my computer!' He uses his computer to help him draw his boats. He's very clever. He can put a picture of a boat on the computer screen and it doesn't look flat at all – you know, it's three-dimensional. Then he can turn it round and round (so he can see what the far side of the boat looks like) and he can even turn it upside down (so he'll know what the boat's bottom looks like).

'You mean Annie has been playing with your computer?'

'No! No!' he was really roaring now. 'Annie couldn't have done this! Annie wouldn't know how to draw a doll's house on the screen and make it spin round and round. Annie's only three years old! No, indeed! Sister did this! Sister's to blame!'

I couldn't believe my ears. Was dad starting to believe Sister was real? Or was he just in one of his rages? When he loses his temper, he says some wild things. But he seems to forget about them later.

'Perhaps Jack knows something about this,' said mum, doubtfully. Jack knows how to work the computer. In fact, Jack knows more about the computer than dad does. When it breaks down, Dad usually has to ask Jack to fix it.

'No, no!' said Dad. 'Jack wouldn't mess about drawing a doll's house. If Jack wanted to play about with the computer, he'd use it to contact America, or Russia, or *Mars!*'

'Tom?' Mum looked doubtfully at me. I can do some things on the computer, but I'm not as good as Jack is.

'No!' Dad was roaring now. 'Some girl did this. Mark my words, Roz, this is more of Sister's work!'

Suddenly there was an echo from across the room. From Walter's cage.

'Hello, Sister!' said the cocky. 'Cup of tea, Sister?'

We all turned to look at Walter. The cocky tipped his head on one side and looked back at us.

Could Walter see Sister?

And what about dad? Did he really believe that Sister was actually able to mess up his computer drawings?

You can never tell when dad's serious. I mean, he always roars around the house when the computer plays up, blaming anyone or anything he could think of – Jack, me, Walter the parrot, the cat.

Once, he'd shouted at mum that her vacuum cleaner had zapped the computer, switched it right off! But when he calmed down, he admitted that the computer had stopped because he'd accidentally pulled the plug out.

This time, when he calmed down, would he forget about blaming Sister?

3

Sister didn't wait very long to cause her next lot of mischief.

It was Saturday morning and mum was in the living room with her old ladies. She has three of them. They are great favourites of hers; she takes them shopping and she drives them round and round the park, and she takes them for picnics in the car. She got to know them through her Meals on Wheels days – these are days when mum drives around and takes hot lunches to people who are too old or too sick to cook for themselves.

This particular Saturday, mum was feeding her old ladies at our place, with banana cake, and pouring tea for them, and getting ready to take them out to buy some new clothes.

Well, Sister soon heard about the banana cake and the new clothes and, of course, Sister wanted some of each.

I guessed there was going to be trouble when I saw Annie making for the living room with an armful of

her own clothes. They were piled up all higgledy-
piggledy and she was dropping stuff as she went. I
tried to pick things up for her but she just shook her
head at me, and walked all over the things she had
dropped.

Mum was very fed up with Annie for bursting into
the living room when she had guests, dragging what
looked like her dirty laundry behind her.

'I'll wash those for you tomorrow, Annie,' she
said. She turned to the old ladies, 'She's very
fussy.'

'No,' said Annie. 'They don't have to be washed.
I'm throwing them out.'

'You are *what*?' Mum's voice sounded gentle
enough, but, if you knew her well, you could tell
that, if Annie really tried, she could get her to lose
her temper – just a little bit.

'Sister doesn't want to wear these any more,' said
Annie firmly. 'Sister says these clothes are junk.'

The old ladies looked puzzled at the mention of
Sister. 'You have another little girl, Mrs Tweedie?'
asked Mrs Tressider.

'No,' said Annie, before mum could get a word in.
'I do. I have a little girl.'

I suppose the old ladies had heard fairy stories
like that before. None of them looked the least bit
surprised.

'And how old is your little girl, Annie?' asked
Miss Quarmby.

'Twenty thirty,' said Annie. Counting is not her

very best thing. She got back to the reason she had
come in to see mum. 'Sister wants us to have some
new stuff.'

'Your little girl wears your clothes, does she,
Annie?' asked Mrs O'Flynn.

'No,' Annie shook her head. I think she's getting
sick of explaining Sister's clothing arrangements.
'She has the same, only *this* big.' She held her hands
out to show Sister's size.

'Well, then,' said Mrs Tressider. 'Sister could
wear your dollies' clothes.'

'Yuck!' Annie shook her head.

'Annie!' Mum spoke quietly but firmly. 'That is
very rude of you.'

'No,' Annie shook her head. 'It wasn't me who
said "yuck". That's what Sister said. I showed her
some of the doll's stuff and Sister said she doesn't
want to wear other people's old clothes.'

'But the Pretty Cherry dolls are just Sister's size,' said mum in her coaxing voice.

'Sister says the Pretty Cherry dolls are dumb,' said Annie. 'She says their eyes look like raisins.'

I said, 'That's because their eyes *are* raisins.' I'd noticed a couple of sad-looking dolls thrown down on the sofa in the family room. They had squashed up raisins where people (and dolls) usually have eyes. I didn't say any more because I suddenly realized this was not a good time to tell mum about this.

'Annie has an invisible friend,' said mum to the ladies. 'And, as Sister always seems to be dressed exactly the same as Annie, I suppose what Annie is saying is that *she* wants some new clothes.'

There goes mum, I thought, explaining things to the grown ups again.

But Mrs O'Flynn didn't seem upset about that. 'I thought as much. Invisible friend, indeed! Oh yes. We had a few of those at our place when my children were young.'

'What's ... in ... fizzable?' asked Annie. She'd heard that word often, since Sister moved in with us.

'Invisible people are people you can't see,' I explained.

'But I can see her!' said Annie, pointing over somewhere behind me. 'She's ...'

Unfortunately, that was the end of the talk about Sister and her clothes because suddenly ...

'BOOM, BOOM, BOOM!'

Loud booming sounds were echoing around the room. The old ladies seemed to rise up off the sofa, with the shock of the sudden noise.

'The clock! The grandfather clock!' Mum's eyes were as wide as saucers.

'BOOM, BOOM, BOOM, BOOM!'

I rushed across to the big clock in the corner. It was the sort that had its own cupboard . . . and half-way up the cupboard there was a window where you could see this big metal thing swinging back and forward. Up above that, was the usual sort of clock face.

'BOOM, BOOM, BOOM!'

And, from the sounds coming out of it, it seemed that somewhere inside it there must be a drum. A very big drum.

The old ladies looked as though someone had stuck their toes into an electric-light socket. Their arms were thrown up in the air. In fact, they looked as though someone had just shouted, 'Stick 'em up!' and waved a gun at them. Their legs were sticking out straight in front of them, and their feet seemed to be wobbling on the end of their legs.

Miss Quarmby, the tiny, thin one, was the first to speak. 'What is it? Gunfire?'

'Yes, what is it mum?' I asked.

'Oh dear,' said mum. She was very flustered. 'I'm afraid the clock is chiming.'

'What's chiming?' asked Annie.

Even when very badly fussed, mum always finds time to explain things to children. 'It's a way old-fashioned clocks had of calling out the time. A lovely, lovely sound of bells.'

'Bells, indeed!' said Mrs Tressider. 'Sounds like the noise builders make when they're blasting holes in the ground.'

'Aren't you supposed to sound a warning whistle before you make a noise like that?' Miss Quarmby's voice sounded very wobbly.

Mum had come over to the clock now, opening up the glass bit where the clock face is. 'I'm so terribly sorry. We silenced it you see, before we brought it home. When my grandfather gave it to us, we realized no one could live in the house with a clock that made so much noise when it...chimed...' Mum was really sticking to her story about the lovely, lovely sound the clock was supposed to be making.

'Chimed!' said Miss Quarmby, in a faint little voice.

'How did your grandfather live with it?' asked Mrs O'Flynn. She had her hands clasped over her ears as though she feared the demon clock would start up again.

'He was a tiny bit deaf,' said mum. 'I think that's why he bought such a loud clock.' She was fiddling around with something inside the clock. She seemed puzzled. And then I saw her look on top of the clock and pick something up. 'Ahhh...here's what I need. This usually fits in here...in the works, you see...it stops the clock from making a noise. Someone must have removed it.'

And then – I could hardly believe this – every single person in that room turned to look at me. Well, when I thought about it later, I guessed they'd worked it out that Annie was too small to reach up and open the glass face of the clock.

But then the weird thing happened. Almost before I knew what I was saying, I found myself shouting, 'Sister did it! Sister's the one!'

I hadn't known I was going to say that. But, as soon as it was out, I knew it was true. The sneaky little thing had climbed up the clock cabinet, opened the clock face (probably working the lock with her teeth), and she'd removed the little piece of wood mum had put in the clock works to stop that awful booming.

'Oh now, Tom!' Mum was shaking her head. 'Don't *you* start blaming things on Sister!'

I couldn't imagine why not. After all, when the computer went bung, Sister was the first one dad blamed! And, even after he calmed down he didn't say anything about having changed his mind.

But they couldn't see this was the same sort of thing. Dad had a talk with me that evening. 'Now look Tom, we know that Annie couldn't have fiddled about with the clock. The key to the cabinet is kept right on top of the clock, and I don't think she could have climbed up there. But you could have, do you see?'

I shook my head. 'I didn't dad, and, anyway, I didn't know the key was kept on top of the cabinet. And I didn't know mum had put the piece of wood in to stop the clock making that loud bonging noise, because I've never *heard* it make that noise before today.'

'Mmmm,' said dad, thinking hard. 'But Annie couldn't have fixed the clock to make that noise, because she simply wouldn't have understood that taking the little piece of wood out would allow the clock to make that hideous noise. Annie, you see, doesn't understand yet how things work. Clocks, videos, and that kind of thing.'

'Computers?' I said. If he was right and Sister could only do what Annie could do, then he'd made a mistake when he accused Sister of drawing a dolls' house on his computer.

He shook his head and laughed. 'All right, Tom, you've got me. I guess when I came into the house shouting that Sister had fiddled with my computer ... well ... I was mad, you see, good and mad ... ' For a moment he didn't seem to know how to go on. 'And I'll have to admit to you, just between the two of us, that I really didn't believe Sister had had anything to do with it.'

'Oh, she did!' I said. 'You were right, dad! I think Sister did fiddle with the computer, and she certainly zapped the clock!'

He shook his head. 'When Annie tells us that Sister has *done* something, we all realize that the truth is Annie has done it herself. Annie has never yet blamed Sister for something which she herself couldn't possibly do.'

Oh dear, they just weren't getting the idea at all. They just didn't understand that there was a bad, bad creature loose in the house.

4

Well, after that, everyone teased me about Sister.

Funnily enough, as time went on, dad seemed to forget all about the day when he had blamed Sister for drawing the dolls' houses on the screen of his computer. He had another talk with me. He said, 'You know, Tom, I can understand why Annie should have this imaginary friend. Lots of small children do, for a bit. But, Tom, you're ten. A little old to be seeing fairies, isn't it?'

I didn't know what to say. I didn't know they had rules about how old you could be when you saw someone nobody else could see. And I hadn't actually seen Sister. But, somehow, I just had the feeling there was someone else in the house with us – someone who loved to make mischief.

And then I had an idea. 'What about the postbox man, dad? He talks to people nobody else can see.'

The postbox man is very well known around our way. He is quite old, and he must be very poor because his shoes have big gaps in them. They leave his toes sitting out in the cold. His clothes are all messy, and he carries his belongings in an old suitcase. The only time he ever puts that suitcase down is when he decides it's time to stop and shout down the slot of a postbox.

Most people get a big shock when they first see him bending down, talking to the letters inside. I'm still not quite used to it. Mum has explained to us that it would be very bad to stare at him and make him feel silly. I don't think she need worry; I don't think the postbox man takes the least notice of people staring at him. I think he's too busy hoping that one day a voice will call back to him from the box.

'Yes,' said dad, 'well, you see, the postbox man is quite a different case.'

'Why?' I asked.

'Well,' said dad, 'when little children start talking to imaginary people, they very often grow out of it. They get bigger, and they forget about their invisible friend, because they have so much fun playing with their real friends.'

Or else they start drawing comic strips so people won't think it's odd that they're fussing about with imaginary people!

'Yes?' I said.

'But the postbox man is quite old now, and I would guess that he doesn't have many friends and he is never going to stop talking into postboxes.'

I nodded, but, you know, I really couldn't see what was so terrible about that. The postbox man seemed quite happy.

Dad had to rush off then. He was late for his Sunday morning tennis game and he hates to miss that.

Jack had been working quietly at his comic strip while dad had been talking to me. He looked up now and said, 'He was trying to tell you the postbox man is bonkers.' He must have seen I looked puzzled. 'You know, funny in the head. Mad!'

Well, why didn't he say so? Grown ups have funny ways of telling you things.

And then a terrible thought hit me. Did dad think I was bonkers, and funny in the head, and mad?

I forgot about that for a moment because there was something I really needed to ask. 'Jack,' I said, 'why are the grown ups so upset because I think Sister is real? I mean, they thought it was great when you used to talk to Mudman, and, although mum and dad have told Annie not to blame things she does on Sister, they really thought it was quite cute when they first found out she had an imaginary friend.'

'Yes,' said Jack. 'But Sister is Annie's very own imaginary friend. They think it's sort of okay for Annie to say she can see her.'

'But not okay for me to say I think she is really here in the house with us?'

Jack twisted about. 'Yes, that's what they think,'

he said. 'You can't really see her, can you?' He looked worried. 'You can't see Sister?'

I didn't want to answer that. I hadn't seen her yet. But I was pretty sure she was somewhere about.

An hour later, I was *really* sure.

Before dad sets out for tennis on a Sunday morning, he always sets the video to record this television programme he specially likes. It's terribly boring; I don't know why he bothers. It's just men and women sitting in chairs for hours and hours talking to one another about money.

Anyway, dad loves that programme.

He came roaring in from tennis, raced over to the television set, fiddled with the video, gave a loud, happy sigh and settled down to watch his programme.

And suddenly there was a loud roar.

I went over to look at the screen of the television set and what I saw gave me a big shock.

Cartoons!

'Tom!' Dad was really roaring. 'Tom, did you change the programming on the video?'

I said, 'No, dad.'

'Tom!' He was really wound up. 'If you wanted to watch the cartoons, while I was out, you could have done so. The video would record my programme while you were watching yours. There was no need to change the programming!'

'But I didn't!'

'Jack. Come out here, Jack!' He was off, questioning the next suspect.

He only had two of us because we were the only ones, beside himself, who could programme the video. Mum said it mucked up when she tried it, and Annie was too small.

We had a lot of trouble convincing dad that neither of us had tampered with the buttons on the video.

'Now, then, Bill,' said mum, in her gentle voice. 'You know the boys wouldn't touch it. They know how much you love that programme. I think, if you'll just calm down, you'll realize that you made a mistake.'

'I *what!*' Dad was roaring at mum now. 'I made a what?'

'You punched the wrong buttons,' said mum.

'Goodness knows, I've done it often enough myself.'

Annie was standing watching the shouting. She knew who had mucked up the video, and so did I.

I went over to her and said, 'Why did Sister do that?'

But Annie didn't answer.

It was no good sharing my suspicions with the rest of them; I'd only get another teasing.

I decided, next Sunday, to sit by the set and watch what happened.

Well, the next week, as soon as dad had taken off for tennis, I saw, out of the corner of my eye, a sudden movement at the top of the bookshelf. I turned quickly and, although I couldn't exactly see what it was, I was sure that a little figure was racing along the top shelf of the bookcase.

I stared hard at the spot where I thought I'd seen something and suddenly there she was, as clear as anything, a tiny little red-haired person, a very small version of Annie, hanging by her fingers from the top shelf of the bookcase. As I watched, she jumped down onto the second top shelf.

And so she clambered right down the bookcase, and made for the big wide shelf at the bottom where the television and the video sit together, with a lead going from one to another.

I hardly dared breathe as I watched her. She looked around and saw a ballpoint pen on the shelf. She scuttled over, picked it up, and sort of tucked it under her arm, with the part that doesn't write sticking out in front of her.

Then she looked around carefully, and backed away from the video, just the way Jack does at footy, when he's going to take a kick at goal.

Then she rushed forward, holding the pen stiff beside her. And, as she got to the video, the end of the pen hit one of the buttons on the video.

So that's how the wicked little creature changed the programming.

I watched as she backed off again, got her pen set, and rushed at the video. Again. And again. And again.

Well, I fixed things that day.

I waited till she'd scuttled along the bottom shelf of the bookcase and began heading for something at the other end.

It was the green people's house, Annie's favourite toy. Mum let her keep it on that shelf so she could play with it in the family room.

It's a little plastic house, with four rooms, and a staircase, and windows and doors and balconies and stuff. And, in its little plastic garden, there were mushrooms for the green people to sit on, and swings for them to swing on, and seesaws for them to go up and down on, and a slippery dip for them to slide down. *You* know, it was the usual sort of toy house that kids have to keep their elves or their pixies or their green people in.

As I watched, Sister went scuttling through the little plastic garden, stopping only to kick a plastic mushroom out of her way. She went through the front door of the house and I heard it slam shut behind her.

So that's where Sister hid when she wasn't plotting mischief with Annie, or tormenting some other member of our family.

Keeping an eye on the little plastic house, I went back to the video, and reset it to dad's programme.

And then, I sat down and thought very hard.

Sister was real, all right. She looked exactly as Annie had said she did. She was dressed in jeans, and a T shirt, and she had trackshoes on her feet, and a ribbon in her hair.

I decided not to tell anyone what I'd seen. And it certainly wasn't a good idea to tell anyone that Sister was living in the green people's house. By the time they went looking for her she would have moved on. To the clock, perhaps. Or the microwave.

I was tired of the teasing, and I didn't want dad and mum to think I was just a copycat, who couldn't imagine his own friend and tried to take over his sister's.

What I had to do was fix things so that everyone could see Sister.

I'd have to set a trap for her.

5

I decided the best place to trap Sister was in the little plastic house. I thought I'd better work fast in case the little green people who lived there figured out a way to toss her out. I was afraid if they got mad enough at her, they would all rush at her and hurl her out into the green plastic garden.

I waited till I was sure Sister had gone out.

Mum and Annie had gone to the supermarket and, of course, she had to be with them. Sister would never miss a chance to ride on the front bar of the supermarket trolley and toss forbidden things into the basket – lollies, and iceblocks on sticks, socks with frilly tops, and the little books they sometimes have in the baskets near the checkouts.

I crept up close to the little plastic house, and listened for sounds of the green people moving around in there. I thought, if I were them, I'd be taking this chance to plan a rebellion, thinking of ways to launch a big attack on the bossy red-headed creature who had moved into their nice, quiet home.

But I couldn't hear anything.

I went over to the place in our kitchen area where mum keeps her roll of clingwrap. You know it; that stretchy stuff you can see through. It sticks to things. Then I got a sharp knife, and mum's kitchen scissors.

When I got back to the green people's house, I listened again, but still there was no noise. Suddenly, I wondered whether this was because the crowd in there would only come to life if Sister were around to annoy them. Or whether it was because whenever she went out they took the chance to have a nap – so they could save up their energy to fight her when she got back.

In case there was anyone awake in there, I whispered, 'You'll thank me for this,' and began my task.

I stuck clingwrap over all the windows (the plastic house has no glass of course, just gaps where the windows ought to be) and over the little doors that lead onto the balconies. The only openings I left clear were the front door (so that Sister could go clattering through it when she came home) and the flat hole at the top of the chimney.

I had a plan. I'd worked it all out very carefully.

But I would need to have all my family in the room to watch it go into action. It wouldn't be the least good forcing Sister to show herself if I was the only one there to see her. It wouldn't even be any good if just Annie were there with me. After all,

Annie had been telling anyone who would listen that she could see Sister already.

Luckily, the table we eat at is very close to the shelf where the green people have their house.

The whole family was sitting at the table, ready to eat, and mum was just serving out the chicken when I noticed a tiny light flickering in one of the windows of the green people's house. They never bothered putting lights on, so I knew Sister was home. Perhaps she was watching the very small television set they have in their living room.

I asked could I leave the table, and, although mum raised her eyebrows, she nodded and said, 'Be quick!'

I scuttled off to Jack's and my room, and fetched my helper.

I'd figured that I needed someone (or something) to help with the trap, and it had to be someone (or something) very small, but a bit scarey.

The budgies were about the right size but we'd already found out they got fits of the shivers when Sister came near them.

So I picked Eric.

Eric is Jack's white mouse. Eric is very small, of course, but lots of people are terrified of him. One day, when mum's old ladies were sitting around in the living room, scoffing hot scones, I'd taken him in to show them. They'd started shrieking. Miss Quarmby had almost fainted when she spotted the little white whiskered face peeping up over my shirt pocket.

I sneaked Eric into the family room and walked quietly over to the little plastic house. I peered at the windows and saw the little light still flickering. I had a look to make sure the clingwrap was still fixed to the windows, and the balcony doors. And I looked at the chimney to see that was still clear.

Then I turned to the table and said, 'Hey, who'd like to see Sister?'

Dad crashed his fork down on the plate and said, 'Tom! Let's not discuss Sister again!' Huh! I think he felt a little bit silly about Sister because of the time he'd lost his temper and shouted out that she'd been messing with his computer! He seemed now to want to forget he'd ever said it.

Mum, of course, was prepared to look. 'Now then, Bill, does it hurt you to go along with Tom, just for once?'

He growled a bit but he said, 'Oh, all right, then. Where is Sister, exactly, Tom?'

I said, 'She's not in sight yet, but she will be in a moment.'

'Tom!' Dad's voice sounded the way it does when big trouble is coming my way. To be exact, when a big whack is coming my way.

'Give him a chance, dad,' said Jack. He's always ready to listen to some new idea. When you tell him about something you'd like to try, he never says, 'But that's impossible!'

'Now, then,' I said. 'If you keep your eyes fixed to the top of the chimney, you will shortly see Sister, as

clearly as you see me. You will see that she is real –
not imaginary, not in the least bit.'

Annie hadn't said anything. She just sat there,
looking pleased and staring at the top of the
chimney.

Dad made a complaining sound. 'Tom, the way
you've been carrying on lately, I'm not sure that I
didn't imagine *you!*'

I crept up towards the house, Eric cuddled in my
left hand. I held him up near my face for a moment
and whispered, 'Kill, Kill!'

Then I thumped on the front door of the little
plastic house with my right hand, shouted 'Police!
Open up!', as loudly as I could, and pushed the door
open.

With my left hand, I pushed Eric inside, and then
I slammed the door shut and stood back so that
everyone at the table could see.

'What on earth!' Dad sounded mad.

'Hush, a moment, Bill!' It's a lucky thing mum is
always so ready to listen to a child's side of things.

I was hoping Sister was like all the older ladies or
girls I knew – afraid of mice! Really, you know, I was
beginning to fear that Sister wasn't afraid of
anything, but luckily that didn't turn out to be
true.

There was a great deal of squealing coming from
the house. I felt sorry for the green plastic ladies. I
mean, they didn't deserve to be frightened out of
their wits by Eric, the fierce white mouse. But I

hoped he would see Sister and decide to give her the biggest scare. I was beginning to think Eric enjoys it when people go squealing and twirling out of his way. Sometimes they even climb up on stools. I suppose they're afraid he'll nibble at their toes with his sharp white teeth.

'What's going on in there?' asked mum.

'I think the green plastic people are trying to climb up on their furniture to get away from Eric,' I said. 'The clattering sound is when they fall off.'

'Oh Tom, you are a very puzzling boy,' said dad sadly. 'Now, it is all very well to have a good imagination. But for ten years you have shown no sign at all that you've got one. Now, suddenly, there's no end to the wild stories you expect us to believe. I ask you! What *are* we to think?'

Well, that was easy. Seeing I was such a sensible boy, such a practical boy, there seemed to be one very obvious thing they could think.

They could think, 'Tom is right!'

I didn't think it would be a good idea to say that, so I said, 'Dad, can't you see the light in the window of the green house?'

Er. Well, yes, he could.

'And can't you hear the noise coming from the green house?'

'Yes, yes!' He sounded very cross.

Well, they all could.

I shouted, 'Go, Eric, go!'

Mum gave a little squeal. 'Eric! Is Eric in there?'

She hadn't seen me put Eric through the door.

And then I turned to the family and said, 'Watch the chimney, watch the chimney!'

And sure enough...

'Here she *comes!*' shouted Jack.

And there was Sister. First, her red head popped up over the top of the chimney. She seemed to be taking a careful look round, as though she thought the whole living room might be alive with killer mice.

Then she seemed to hoist herself up, and for a moment, she stood on top of the chimney, and we all saw her, as clearly as anything, her little pointy face alive with mischief, her red hair tied back with green ribbons, her blue overalls and red and white striped sweater an exact copy of the ones Annie was wearing that day.

Jack looked stunned. 'Mum! Dad! It's Sister! Tom was right! Annie was right! She's really there!'

'Oh my sainted aunt!' said dad.

'I can see her!' said mum. 'Oh, what a darling!'

'Hello, Sister!' croaked Walter, peering at her from his cage.

'Sister!' It was Annie shouting. 'Don't worry, Sister. I'm coming!'

And before I could stop her, Annie was across the room, she'd snatched Sister up in her hand and was streaking for the back door.

By the time we all caught up with them, Sister had disappeared again.

'Where's she gone?' I shouted.

Annie pointed to the table on the patio. 'She's there! Can't you see her?'

But none of the rest of us could. Not any longer.

'Well, Tom,' said dad. 'I must admit you were absolutely right. Sister has been in the house with us all along.' With that, he headed off towards his garden workroom.

'He's going to ask the computer what to do about her,' said mum. 'And you two boys can come back inside and catch Eric. I don't want to touch him; I'm afraid Tom may have given him the killer instinct.'

As we searched for the little mouse, Jack and I worked things out. While Annie could see Sister all the time, the rest of us could see her only when she was up to the worst of her mischief – such as resetting the video to record the cartoons. Or when she was in some kind of trouble – such as being chased up a chimney by a wild animal.

'You were lucky, with Eric, though,' Jack said. 'She could just as easily have scared the life out of *him*!'

'Oh, no,' I said. 'Eric has got the killer instinct. He got psyched up the day he went for Miss Quarmby.'

This is true. Eric seems to feel very powerful since he got loose in the plastic house; Jack thought he should give him a lot of warm milk to calm him down. He seems to sit in his box, his whiskers quivering, wondering who to terrorize next.

Well, now here's how things stood.

Everyone now knew that Sister was real.

Everyone knew that it was a case of 'Now you see her; now you don't.'

Everyone but *Annie* thought Sister was rather a pest.

Oh, that should be everyone but Annie and *Eric* thought Sister was rather a pest.

Jack thinks Eric is just waiting for the day he gets a chance to chase her again. 'So,' said Jack, 'Eric doesn't think she's a pest, Eric thinks she might make a very good lunch.'

'Do mice eat people?' I asked. Jack does seem to know such interesting things.

'Mostly they don't,' said Jack. 'But then mostly mice do not get a chance to chase someone so close to their own size.' I had quite a think about that.

Because we still had to figure out what to do about the tiny red-headed terrorist who was messing up our lives.

6

Jack had been thinking very hard. Jack's way of thinking is to sit with a pen in his hand, drawing furiously in the little squares of his comic strip. He fills in picture after picture, without speaking or looking up.

You know, I've been watching him very closely lately, and I'm absolutely sure Jack doesn't know what is going to come up in each square of the comic until after the picture is finished. It's as though Telquark and the star fleet people and the Trogs all do exactly as they like in that comic strip. All they need Jack for is to hold the pen steady.

At last, Jack spoke. Or maybe what I was hearing were the words of the star fleet commander coming out past Jack's teeth. 'Telquark thinks we should deal with Sister the same way he fights the Trogs.'

'You mean we should have a never-ending war with her?' I asked. That sounded quite tiring.

And not a very good idea. After all, Telquark has been blasting away at the Trogs ever since Jack was old enough to make marks on a piece of paper with a pencil. And the Trogs are still troggling.

'Should we fire at her with a Trogblaster?' I asked. 'Or could he design a special Sisterblaster for us?'

But Jack didn't answer. He just kept on drawing. Well, I suppose, from Jack, that is an answer.

Suddenly, I noticed something alarming. 'You're drawing Sister!' I shouted, as he reached for a red pen to ink in the little horror's fiery curls. 'How did she get in your comic strip?'

Well, I suppose that was a silly question. Sister probably heard Jack and me talking about Telquark's suggestion that we declare war on her. And, of course, the first thing she'd do, in a case like that, would be to leap into the comic strip and set about annihilating the brave space fleet commander.

'He shouldn't have spoken so loudly,' I said.

'It was you who did all the shouting,' said Jack.

I leaned over his shoulder, so I could see what Sister was doing.

She had wrestled Telquark out of his seat at the spaceship computer and appeared to be clacking away at the keyboard. The seat was too low for her, of course, so she was standing on it, brought up to the right level by a pile of manuals.

'Now that she's overpowered Telquark,' Jack said calmly, 'she's getting ready to take control of the star fleet. But first she has to plot a new course.'

'Where's she thinking of heading for?' I asked.

Jack shook his head. 'From the look on Telquark's face, I don't think it's anywhere near – or anywhere nice. I think she's going to send him and his fleet on a one-way journey to the farthest reaches of space!'

Whew! When Sister picks on someone, she really gives them a walloping. And, apart from giving Jack just that one little piece of advice about declaring war on her, Telquark had never done a thing to Sister. It could have been that she was terrorizing him just because he was the first person she'd seen that day.

'Why doesn't he just push her off his chair and tell her to mind her own business?'

Jack rolled his eyes. 'I think he's hoping it will take her a while to figure out how to use the computer. It's a 30th-century state-of-the-art Intergalactic, you know. It took him three light years just to figure out how to turn it on.'

Now, Jack had told me often that the spaceship computer is very complicated. It has to be, to send a star fleet whirling through deep space, and it's not supposed to let it smack into anything – planets or comets or space rubbish.

'Telquark thinks,' said Jack slowly (his voice was beginning to sound strange, far away), 'that, even after Sister figures out how to use the computer, working out the new course will take her so long that he'll have time to think of a way to get rid of her.'

'Huh!' I said. 'It will take her about two frames of your comic strip to figure out how to work that computer, and one more to plot the course, and then she'll be looking round for somebody new to torment.'

'Yes,' and Jack, in his new eerie voice, 'but don't you see? While she's busy in the comic strip she's leaving the real world alone. For instance, she hasn't belted Walter's bell in ages.'

That was true. Sister loves to torment the cocky by sneaking up behind him and kicking his bell. Of course, he belts the bell a bit himself but that's okay. That way, he's expecting the noise and doesn't fall off his perch with shock. I suddenly realized that Walter had been able to live in peace now for nearly half an hour.

'And it's been nearly an hour since the grandfather clock went bong!'

Just then, we had an interruption. Annie came bustling in and leaned against Jack's left arm. She showed no surprise at seeing Sister in the comic strip. I was positive someone had already told her. Maybe Sister had sent her a message through the air.

She watched Jack draw Sister at the spaceship computer. 'Sister says she'll be finished with that silly toy in a few minutes. Sister says she wants to go out and play now.'

'What?' I said. 'But the spaceship is in orbit over the Trog planet.' Sister hadn't sent the fleet off yet on its doomed voyage into deep space but I felt the time for a blast off must be getting close. 'Are you sure she wants to leap out now?' As soon as I said that, I realized I'd asked a silly question. Sister wouldn't be likely to go off with Telquark on his space exile.

'Hurry up!' said Annie. 'Yes, Sister says open the door of the spaceship now; she wants to jump on those people's heads.'

'Who's heads?'

'Those Trugs things,' said Annie. 'Sister says . . .'

'They're Trogs,' said Jack, in his eerie flat voice. 'And they eat people like Sister for breakfast.'

'Sister says they won't eat her. Sister says they wouldn't dare.'

'Let her go,' I said. 'Let's see how Sister handles the dangerous, person-eating Trogs.'

Sister handled them very well. And very quickly. Annie and I watched closely as Jack drew the next three comic-strip squares.

Sister didn't waste a second being scared of the Trogs. She just called them all out from behind their rocks and lined them up. She seemed to be shouting at them – stamping up and down in front of them, waving her arms about, and roaring. The Trogs were so big they had to peer down somewhere between their toes to see where the voice was coming from.

'They're standing up straighter,' I said.

'Sister says those Trugs are a mess,' said Annie

happily. 'Sister says she'll soon show them how to fight.'

'Fight who?' I asked, anxiously.

'You mean fight *whom*?' said a gentle voice behind me. I hadn't heard mum come into the room. It seemed she'd noticed a strange atmosphere in the house. It had taken her a moment or two to realize it was something she often asks for but hadn't experienced for a while – peace and quiet. Naturally she'd been extremely alarmed by it, and had come looking for us to see what sort of mischief we were up to.

'Sister is going to help the Trogs fight Telquark,' said Jack.

'I thought we liked Telquark,' said mum.

'*We* do,' I said. I turned to Jack. 'Hang on! How can the Trogs fight him if Sister's sent him and his star fleet out into the far reaches of space?'

'She's going to help the Trogs chase him.'

'What in?' I said. The most the Trogs had managed in the way of flight vessels so far was a wooden aeroplane sent up in the air with a rubber band.

Annie had the answer to that one. 'Sister says the Trugs need some spaceships, really quickly. Sister says she knows how to make them. Sister is drawing them now, just like dad draws his boats.'

'Designing them, you mean?' I asked.

'Ummmm ... ' she said. 'Yes, like that.'

'How?' I said. 'The Trugs ... Trogs ... have no computer.'

The answer to that one was very quick in coming.

First we heard a roar from the back garden. Then we heard a door bang – the door of dad's workroom. Then we heard another door bang – the back door of the house.

Then dad was with us, snorting and spitting fire.

'Who in tarnation is fiddling with my computer?'

'Is it showing the design of a spaceship?' I asked.

Dad stopped. 'I'm not sure what it is, at this point. But there are calculations whizzing down the screen, columns and columns of figures. It could be the plans for a spaceship; or it could be someone's idea for a very fancy new electronic kettle.'

'I think you'll find your answer here,' mum pointed at the comic strip. Her finger was resting just near the square Jack was filling in. There was Sister, sitting on a rock, surrounded by adoring Trogs, picking away at a tiny portable keyboard. No doubt it was transmitting instructions to dad's computer in the little building in our backyard.

Dad rushed out to see whether Sister had started to send actual drawings through.

We heard another yell, followed by the two doors banging and he was back with us again. 'It *is* a spaceship of some kind. She's got it up in three dimensions now, turning it round and round on the screen.'

But that wasn't all. It seemed when dad got out to his office, he found stuff coming through on his Fax machine – it was churning out page after page of orders for hammers and nails and drills and welding rods and some other instruments that dad had never heard of.

'Get her out of that comic strip at once!' said dad.

But he quietened down when we explained to him that we thought it was important to keep Sister busy with the Trogs. 'Yes, Bill. Let her blow up their planet,' mum took a gloomy view, it seems, 'and leave ours in one piece.'

He shook his head. 'Will nothing stop her?'

Suddenly Jack made a funny little noise in his throat.

'What is it?' asked mum.

'I think he needs chocolate, mum,' I said. 'To keep his strength up. It's very tiring for him, you know, receiving these images from the Trog planet and putting them down on paper for us to see.'

Jack took the chocolate gratefully. In fact, we all had some. Chocolate mice, they were. Mum keeps a box of them for special treats.

And that's when something seemed to go wrong. Jack picked up his pen again, but somehow he didn't seem to be getting any inspiration.

For a moment, he drew nothing.

And then, suddenly it seemed as though his motor started up again. But this time, all he drew in the new square was a giant eye. It filled the entire frame.

'Whose eyeball is that, Jack?' asked dad, munching his mouse.

Jack shook his head. 'I don't know. All I can tell you is it's a creature so large that one of his eyes fills the entire square. Look!'

In the next frame, one eye filled the entire sky. We could see the Trogs running for the shelter of the rocks. Even Sister took a moment to glance up.

'Yaah!' The shriek came from Annie. She got up and sped towards the door, but mum stopped her by a lucky grab at the seat of her jeans.

'What's wrong with you, Annie?'

'It's The Great Mouse!' shivered Annie. 'The biggest most fiercest creature in the world!'

'Is Sister afraid of the Great Mouse?' I asked.

'Yaaaaahhhh!' It seemed anyone in their right mind is afraid of the Great Mouse. The Great Mouse eats tall buildings at a single gulp.

'Calm down, Annie!' said dad. 'Sister can handle this. Sure, she's fighting Telquark and the star fleet *as well* as the Great Mouse, but she's got the Trogs to help her.'

To me, that seemed about as good as having the budgies to help her.

'How did the Great Mouse happen to wander by?' I asked Jack. He looked better now that he'd had something to eat. Chocolate can be a great help when you're feeling tired.

'Telquark managed to call him up on the radio,' said Jack.

'You mean Telquark is friendly with the Great Mouse?'

No, no one is friendly with the Great Mouse, it seems, but Telquark sent him an unsigned message: WARNING! DANGEROUS EARTHLING HAS JUST CAPTURED THE PLANET OF THE TROGS. IS NOW BUILDING HER OWN STAR FLEET AND SAYS SHE'S COMING AFTER YOU, SO HOW DO YOU LIKE THAT YOU BIG BULLY MOUSE?

'Telquark is still within radio range of the Trog planet, then?' I asked. I thought he and his fleet would be out beyond the reaches of our universe by now.

'He's been working at the computer,' Jack was drawing the scene as he spoke. 'He's figured out how to cancel Sister's instructions. He's in orbit over the Trog planet. He's waiting to see what the Great Mouse does to Sister and the Trogs. If they've got any fight in them by the time the Mouse has finished, he's going to send his fighter ships in with their Trogblasters and give them all a jolly good fright.'

'What's that noise?' mum asked. 'It sounds as though a star war has broken out in the living room.'

'It's Sister!' said Annie, darting for the door. 'She wants us to see what she's doing.'

'It's the television set!' shouted dad, following Annie. 'It's switched itself on! What next? What *next*!'

Sure enough! There, on our television screen, was the war between Sister and the Great Mouse. The Trogs were hurling rocks up into the sky and she was blasting away with a ray gun. 'That belongs to Telquark,' I said. 'She must have taken it from the space closet in the spaceship.'

We got a nice close-up of the Great Mouse, floating about in the sky, pink and white and huge and evil. 'He looks like Eric,' said Jack. He'd brought his comic strip with him, and was sketching quickly.

Now, on the screen, we saw Sister pointing to a tall, skinny tree. In no time, the Trogs had cut it down and stripped the branches off it ... Then she came running out of the bush with a long trailing vine. She must have cut it specially.

'She's making a giant bow and arrow,' I said. 'Watch her!'

'Yes, Sister is going to make the arrows next,' said Annie. 'Sister says it won't take a minute once she explains to those dopey Trugs how to do it ... '

Things had begun to look a little scary for the Great Mouse. Sister soon had her Trog army taking aim at the sky with their giant bow and arrow. She had Trogs at each end of the tree part, bending the ends back and holding them steady. And in the centre of the bow and arrow she had a long line of them (each one holding on to the waist of the Trog in front of him) ready to pull the vine back, while holding the blunt end of the arrow.

The Trogs at each end of the bent tree would hold

on tight, while the Trog line holding on to the vine and the arrow would suddenly let go both at once, and the arrow would shoot up into the air and hit the giant creature. Of course, if the Trog line got it wrong and forgot to let go of the arrow, they might go whizzing up into the air after it, and the Great Mouse would eat them.

They actually did lose a few hundred Trogs that way, but after that the ones who were left seemed to get the hang of it.

But the Great Mouse moved about surprisingly quickly for such a huge blobby creature. As the arrows came up, he wriggled out of their way.

'I wonder how Telquark's doing?' I said.

There was a burst of laughter from the kitchen area. Mum had gone over there to heat up some food. We all turned to see what was amusing her.

'The microwave!' she bubbled. 'When I turned it on, the door lit up like a television screen. It's a transmission from Telquark's star fleet!'

'Good grief!' said dad. 'Don't turn anything else on! No radiators! No electric jugs! If we get any more electricity loose around here we might find the whole house shooting up into the air and off into space!'

We all rushed out to the kitchen area to see what Telquark was doing. The microwave had no sound, of course, but that problem was soon solved.

'Telquark to star fleet! Come in star fleet!' The voice was coming from Walter's cage. It rattled on and on, in the parrot's squawky voice, instructing the star fleet to fly low over the Trog landscape and fire their Trogblasters at Sister and her troops.

Jack was rushing from one end of the family room to the other. From the television showing the scene on the Trog planet, to the microwave showing Tel-quark at work on his spaceship, he couldn't draw fast enough to get it all into the comic strip.

'Don't worry, Jack, if you can't keep up,' said dad, pointing at the video. Its 'Record' light was glowing. 'I see Sister has kindly switched that on, in case we were out and missed the scene of her great victory.' He paused. 'I assume she's going to win?'

By hook or by crook, Sister is going to win, even if it takes her the next four centuries to do it.

Jack stayed with the microwave now for a bit, recording the battle preparations.

Dad kept watch on the video, ready to put in a new tape whenever the old one ran out. Finally, the battle scene faded from the television and the microwave, Walter stopped squawking, and fell into a deep exhausted sleep, the computer in dad's office shut down, and the Fax machine ground to an exhausted halt.

'Is the battle over?' asked mum.

'No,' said Annie. 'It's just night time on the Trug's planet. They've all gone to sleep.'

'You mean we have to go through this every day?' asked dad.

'Oh yes, dad. I hope so,' said Jack. 'Can we leave the video running?'

'No need,' said dad. 'Sister programmes it from the Trog planet. It seems to switch on whenever she wants it to.'

Annie had the latest news bulletin from the tiny space terrorist. 'Sister says she's going to blast the Great Mouse out of the sky ...'

'What with? That bow and arrow?' I scoffed.

'Yes, and then she's going to build the Trug's spaceship and *then* she's going to chase Telquark and his star fleet to the edge of space, and then...'

'And then she's going to have dinner,' said dad. 'And so are we! Right, Roz?'

Well, that was the last we saw of Sister. In person, I mean. It seems to be taking rather longer than she thought to finish off the Great Mouse.

She's still appearing in Jack's comic strip, of course. Frightening the living daylights out of aliens, tangling with extra-terrestrials, mugging Mudman, terrorizing Telquark, forcing the slobby old Trogs to go jogging, so they'll be strong enough to help her conquer the universe.

Mum explained it all to us. 'You see, Sister just needed something interesting to *do,* really. I think she got quite bored, just lolling around the house, waiting for a chance to mess things up for us.'

'It was fun, though,' said dad, 'Having her here.' He added quickly. 'Of course, some of the things she did were simply not *allowed.* But still, Sister had a certain whomp about her!'

It's certainly quieter at our place without her.

It's sort of nice, though, for us all to sit down and look at the new drawings in Jack's comic strip each evening, just before Annie has to go to bed, and find out what Sister and Telquark and the Trogs and the Great Mouse have been up to in that day's instalment of the never-ending war.

Go, *Sister*!

About the author

Joan Flanagan has worked as a newspaper humorist, a film and book publicist, public servant, literary reviewer and advertising copywriter before she started writing children's books from her Sydney terrace house.

Her children's books include *The Dingbat Spies, Rose Terrace, The Squealies, The Ghost in The Gazebo,* and the picture books *Blinks* and *Mr Shanahan's Secret.*

About the illustrator

Bill Wood was born in Whyalla, South Australia, in 1966. He graduated from Underdale College in Adelaide with a Bachelor of Design degree in 1987. Ever since he can remember, Bill has loved drawing. He enjoys capturing the humour in people and circumstances. Now a freelance illustrator and designer living in Melbourne, he has illustrated two children's picture books – *Angus Thought He Was Big* and *Where is The Lion?*

The Dingbat Spies

When 'Tangletoes' Latimer announces that
the family are moving house, his wife escapes
hastily to Budapest, the housekeeper resigns,
and the pet budgie flies away. So the moving
is left to his long-suffering children and the
extraordinarily untalented rock group, The
Fallen Angels, which Latimer manages.

But the new house is no ordinary house – the
toaster talks, there are secret passages,
mysterious telephones in strange places, and
computers that issue the oddest information.
Not to mention the strange uniformed
neighbours who move into their house in the
depths of the night ...

Rose Terrace

Why does Sophie keep waking up, terrified by the same nightmare? And why is it that the things that happen in these hideous dreams are being enacted, at the same moment, in a place on the other side of the city? Can you be a ghost without knowing it?

Luckily for Sophie, there are friends only too willing to solve the puzzle. And when they do, Sophie finds she has been granted her most secret wish.

HEARD ABOUT THE PUFFIN CLUB?

... it's a way of finding out more about Puffin books and authors, of winning prizes (in competitions), sharing jokes, a secret code, and perhaps seeing your name in print! When you join you get a copy of our magazine, *Puffinalia,* sent to you four times a year, a badge and a membership book.

For details of subscription and an application form, send a stamped addressed envelope to:

The Australian Puffin Club
Penguin Books Australia Limited
P.O. Box 257
Ringwood
Victoria 3134

and if you live in the UK, please write to

The Puffin Club Dept A
Penguin Books Limited
Bath Road
Harmondsworth
Middlesex UB7 ODA

FOR THE BEST PAPERBACKS, LOOK FOR THE

PUFFIN

Books by Joan Flanagan in Puffin

The Dingbat Spies

When 'Tangletoes' Latimer announces that the family are moving house, his wife escapes hastily to Budapest, the housekeeper resigns, and the pet budgie flies away. So the moving is left to his long-suffering children and the extraordinarily untalented rock group, The Fallen Angels, which Latimer manages.

But the new house is no ordinary house—the toaster talks, there are secret passages, mysterious telephones in strange places, and computers that issue the oddest information. Not to mention the strange uniformed neighbours who move into their house in the depths of night . . .

Rose Terrace

Why does Sophie keep waking up, terrified by the same nightmare? And why is it that the things that happen in these hideous dreams are being enacted, at the same moment, in a place on the other side of the city? Can you be a ghost without knowing it?

Luckily for Sophie, there are ingenuous friends (old and new) only too willing to solve the puzzle. And when they do, Sophie finds she has been granted her most secret wish.

The Squealies

Michael Furley is a perfectly ordinary nine-year-old—except that he can make rain, and flap his arms and fly.

Michael only has to stand still for a minute and strange troublesome creatures come flocking to his side—a fierce, furry animal with its feet on backwards; a strange flat boy who's been imprisoned for eighty years in a mirror; and a spaceship crammed with squealing extra-terrestrial wimps, who can't find their way home.

The Squealies is an extraordinary collection of stories about extra-terrestrial creatures and the highly eccentric family who must cope with them.

FOR THE BEST PAPERBACKS, LOOK FOR THE

PUFFIN

Elmer the Rat

Elmer was a rat, a very hungry rat, who lived on the Sydney waterfront. At home there was never enough to eat, so Elmer would spend most of his time on the docks, where there were pie crusts and prawn heads and bits of things left in tins. There were also odd boots and coils of rope to curl up and sleep in, and of course his mates, the seagulls.

Every day Elmer watched the ships wallowing up and down the harbour, leaving trails of delicious bits of cabbage and chips and sausage. Where did all the food come from? The seagulls thought they knew and they told him. So Elmer stowed away on a ship to find The Other Place and scampered right into trouble.

Ships' rats with wicked teeth, sailors with boots and knives—they were all out to stop him. And The Other Place had a few shocks waiting for him too.

Elmer Makes a Break

Elmer the rat lived on the waterfront where life was hungry and dangerous. Then builders pulled down his wharf and put up Mother Murphy's Fishburgers Take Away. The rats moved in, and there was nothing to do but eat.

Elmer wanted to escape the soft life and live on his jungle instincts. But outside waited savage cats, huge white rats, cunning scientists, strange puzzles and mazes. They had plans for Elmer, and some of them were shocking.

Elmer Runs Wild

Elmer the rat lived in Mother Murphy's Fishburgers Take Away. Life was good. Then Mother Murphy's started to sell nothing but squid—no more golden fatty fish fingerettes or half-finished buckets of greasy french fries, just squid. One night Mother Murphy's caught fire and burned down. Elmer took to the bush.

What did he find? A crazy fox, an angry snake, silly sheep, a helpful koala, mad dogs, bushfires and floods, and a surprising new friend.

No wonder Elmer ran wild.

Books by Barbara Giles in Puffin

Bicycles Don't Fly

Why don't bicycles fly?

Jack, champion billycarter, thinks he has the answer. When he gets a bike for Christmas, adventures begin, with bandits and chases, races and rewards—and trouble from Pug.

Then Jack enters the biggest billycart race ever. With Bill to help him, and Pug out to win no matter what, can he win? But Mary Lou, and her new Formula M.L. Mark I, is a real threat.

After the race, Jack starts thinking again about those flying bicycles.

Flying Backwards

Jack longs for a BMX bike so he can compete with his friends, Mary Lou and Dib. His dad says no.

The summer holidays begin and everyone is away—except for Pug. Making the best of things, the boys set off together for a day's ride on their old bikes. But Old Bill's magic bicycle oil is up to its old tricks and they find themselves flying back in time—and into the old goldmining town of Skewe, where Pug has a lucky find. Perhaps the boys will get their BMX bikes after all.

But first of all they must get back into the twentieth century—and that doesn't prove so easy.

FOR THE BEST PAPERBACKS, LOOK FOR THE

PUFFIN

Alex is My Friend

Angelica is lonely when they move to an isolated house in the country. Her father is busy writing his books, her mother has gone away and they never see her.

Then (did the house help?) she finds the diary written by Alex more than fifty years earlier. It is like having a friend to stay in the house who knows things to do and places to go, secrets of all sorts, though there's one secret that even Alex won't tell. Because of Alex, Angelica gets to know more and more people, exciting things happen and when she and her father decide to hold a house-having party, the house is full of friends.

Bill

'What's Bill going to do?' she said. 'Oh Alice, what am I going to do about Bill?'

It's the Depression and times are hard. Bill's Dad has gone up north, trudging the roads, trying to find work. So, when Bill's Mum suddenly falls ill there's nowhere for Bill to go—except up the country to his Grandpa whom he has never met.

Bill works hard on the farm. He knows his Grandpa doesn't want him and he's lonely. But things look up when he goes to school and finds a mate—until there's trouble. Then comes the big storm and Bill knows he must get help . . .

FOR THE BEST PAPERBACKS, LOOK FOR THE

PUFFIN

Regina's Impossible Dream
Judith Worthy

Regina remembered the cage in the egg-laying shed. She'd been much safer there to be sure. No men with axes, no dogs, no foxes or terrors swooping from the sky.

But in the egg-laying shed the sun never shone. There was no rain, no dust, no green grass; nowhere to make a comfortable nest. It was not a bit like the perfect farm in the Impossible Dream.

Other battery hens dreamed the Impossible Dream but only Regina managed to escape and wander the countryside in search of the farm.

Is the Dream really Impossible?

Flocks' Socks and Other Socks
Michael Dugan
Illustrated by Peter Viska

Grubby Wilbur Flocks is just one of the many weird and wonderful people you will meet in this collection of nonsense verse by popular children's author, Michael Dugan.

You'll meet a few old favourites, like Billy, the most horrible boy in the world, Aunt Ella Grumpling, and Rumbletum Rapples, and you'll find out about zany new creations like a man-eating fridge, magic sneezes, a foul-mouthed parrot, musical goldfish, a flying clothesline, and a host of other extraordinary things.

The Undoing of Jeremy Kite
Maureen Stewart

John Smith knew he was boring. He had never done anything adventurous in his whole life—that was, until he met Henrietta Hannah Heaven.

Jeremy Kite knew he was different; he was definitely not boring and not particularly nice. Almost from the day he was born he had a strange look on his face as if he didn't approve of what he saw. But after twelve years of Jeremy Kite, his parents decided they had had enough.

Books by Helen Hunt in Puffin

The Puffin Book of Australian Reptiles

In this book you will find out about Australian reptiles from A to Z. Snakes, lizards, crocodiles, geckos, tortoises and more are described, each one identified with a drawing or colour photograph. Helen Hunt tells about the different species, where they live, what they eat, which ones are dangerous and which are not, and how you can study them safely. She also explains many of the myths and superstitions that surround these creatures and helps to separate fact from fiction.

The Puffin Book of Australian Spiders

In this book you will find out about Australian spiders from A to Z. Not just spiders, but mites, ticks and scorpions are also described. All are members of the arachnid family. Helen Hunt identifies each one with a drawing or colour photograph, tells about the different types, where they live, how they make their webs, what they eat, and which ones are dangerous. She points out which ones you can find wherever you live in Australia, and explains how you can study them safely.

Arranged alphabetically, and with an index, these books are a must for all children who want to share Helen Hunt's fascination with and understanding of Australia's natural world.